Recipes from History -

Conten

Introduction	1
Chocolate- Drinks	5
To Make Chocolate with Water (1723)	6
To Make Wine Chocolate (1723)	7
How to Make Chocolate (1774)	8
Sham Chocolate (1774)	9
Chocolate - Food	11
Macreuse en ragout au Chocolat (1693) (Duck stew with chocolate)	12
Chocolate Biscuits (1749)	13
A Chocolate Tart (1787)	14
To Make a Tourte de Chocolate (1781)	15
To Make Chocolate Puff (1786)	16
To Make Chocolate Cream (1800)	17
To Frittura che potra servire da grasso, e da magro (Chocolate-battered omelette) (18th Century)	· 18
Zuppa cioccolatata (Chocolate Soup) (18th Century)	19
Notes	20
Authors' Info	21
Acknowledgments	21
Bibliography	22

The
Copper Pot

www.thecopperpot.co.uk

Introduction

Recipes from History is a series of booklets that will hopefully encourage the reader to delve into the sights, smells and tastes of the past through a range of historic recipes presented for the modern kitchen. We have tried to stay as honest as possible to the original recipes, only changing things when an ingredient is not readily available today, or when tastes have changed in a way that would make a dish completely unpalatable to the modern diner, such as the amount of butter or fat.

There are many books available that present historic recipes, but often they do not tell you what the original recipe was, or where it came from. With *Recipes from History* you can see the original recipe and learn a little about how that recipe may have been used.

— 〰〰〰 —

Chocolate has long been much loved, but it has not always been enjoyed in the bars that are so ubiquitous across the world today. Until the mid-1800s you would have primarily encountered chocolate as a drink or perhaps as an ingredient in certain food dishes.

Throughout this book we present some of the common and obscure chocolate recipes from the late 1600s through until the early 1800s. However, before delving into the culinary history of chocolate it is also worth spending some time exploring how chocolate first arrived into Europe, how it was perceived and also how it came to be used and consumed in Britain.

— 〰〰〰 —

One of the earliest recorded encounters with chocolate by a European was in 1565, when Girolamo Benzoni described it as "being more a drink for pigs than for humanity". This strange drink encountered by the conquistadors was later said to be "somewhat bitter" and that "it satisfies and refreshes the body but does not inebriate".

This was the local drink of *cacahuatl*, made from the seeds of the cacao tree, domesticated some 3,000 years previously by the Olmecs. It had been drunk progressively by the Olmecs, Maya and Aztecs, by pounding the fermented seeds and mixing them with chilli, vanilla and water. This drink was frothed by pouring it from one cup to another, and normally drunk tepid. Cacahuatl was said to posses mystical properties and was an important element of many pre-Columbian American religious beliefs as well as being used as money or taxes as part of their social and economic systems.

The Spanish did take to chocolate and soon referred to it as "the healthiest thing", and they appreciated chocolate's qualities as a stimulant. They then added another exotic ingredient from the other side of the world to improve the taste – sugar, and served it hot with their breakfast for its energy boost.

Chocolate remained primarily as a drink for the following 200 years, but it is was the centre of a major debate for a long period as the Spanish church could not decide whether it was a food or a drink, and this affected whether it could be consumed on fast days. It was a drink that functioned like a food, and often contained many food-like ingredients, such as bread crumbs or eggs.

The Spanish brought chocolate to Spain from Central America, where it was initially consumed by the aristocracy. The drink was time consuming to make and used expensive and exotic ingredients. Chilli and vanilla were still used from America, but orange was being introduced as a flavour. Demand for the "chocolate nut tree" was increasing and large plantations were spreading throughout their empire from the West Indies to the Philippines.

During the 1600s chocolate began to spread from Spain into Italy and France. After a slow and uncertain start, by the 1680s, chocolate was being drunk by almost all of the European royal elite. The Spanish Infanta Maria Teresa had married King Louis XIV of France bringing the drink firmly into the French court.

The English were a little slow on the uptake of chocolate, and the earliest encounters are likely to have been via privateers seizing cargos of cacao beans whilst hunting the seas for Spanish gold. Occasionally valuable cargoes of the ugly brown lumps were burnt, not realising their value. But, by the mid 1600s chocolate had joined coffee and tea as one of the desirable stimulant drinks, and it is recorded by Samuel Pepys in 1660.

Sir Hans Sloane was an important Englishman in our history of chocolate as he is said to have introduced the idea of drinking chocolate with milk. In fact milk was used with chocolate prior to this period. Having described chocolate to be "nauseous" whilst living in Jamaica as a physician and naturalist, Sloane developed his own more palatable recipe, made with milk, which was later sold to the Cadbury family.

Chocolate by the 1700s was still predominantly a drink. The Spanish flavours were changing with the chilli being replaced with the more easily obtained long pepper, and the citrus element being provided with cardamom. Chocolate houses had reinforced its popularity throughout Europe and it was being drunk from London to Venice for breakfast and in the evenings while gambling.

We see English recipe books of the 18th century referring to both chocolate cakes or bars, as well as cocoa nuts, suggesting that processed chocolate was available to the middle classes, as well as seeing the raw nut being processed in the home. Chocolate starts to venture into foodstuffs during this period as a flavouring. The recipes are frequently rich and creamy and would have graced the second course of a Georgian dinner table, or the dessert course.

It is not until 1847 that the technique of processing chocolate further into the chocolate bar was developed by J.S Fry and Sons, and powdered milk was created by Henri Nestlé in 1867, which was then blended into chocolate in 1879, giving us milk chocolate.

— ∿∿∿∿ —

We hope you enjoy exploring these historic chocolate recipes as much as we have enjoyed researching and recreating them.

Suzi and Nick

3

Chocolate Drinks

If you were offered a 'chocolate' prior to the 19th century, in all probability you were actually being offered a drink of chocolate. Hot chocolate began its European life as a Spanish drink, having been imported from Central America. However, it quickly spread throughout Europe, first amongst the aristocracy and then through to the middling folk. There was even a 'Sham Chocolate' recipe (p. 9) for those who could not gain access to the real thing!

By the mid-1600s, in places like Venice, London and Paris, chocolate was in the height of its popularity and was drunk in chocolate and coffee houses, primarily by men. For women, it was a drink to be enjoyed in the home, especially going into the 1700s.

In the 1600s you were as likely to find chocolate made with water as you were to find it made with milk, or indeed half milk and half water. The recipe on p.6 'To make chocolate with water' illustrates that although chocolate was increasingly being drunk with milk, it was still made with water. This is by no means the only recipe giving instructions on how to make chocolate with water, so it was presumably still a common occurrence.

People were making their chocolate drinks with more than just chocolate, water (or milk) and sugar throughout the late 1600s and 1700s. Spices such as cinnamon, pepper and nutmeg were often used to replace the traditional chilli of the Aztec/Spanish chocolates, as in the recipe 'How to Make Chocolate' (p.8). Thickeners were also used, such as ground nuts, eggs and cream.

Experimentation with chocolate drinks was also taking place, as can be seen by John Nott's delicious recipe 'To Make Wine Chocolate' on p.7. It did not take people long to discover the wonderful pairing of chocolate and port!

To Make Chocolate with Water

To a Quart of Water, put a quarter of Pound of Chocolate without Sugar, fine Sugar a quarter of a Pound, good Brandy a quarter of a Pound, fine Flour half a quarter of an Ounce, a little Salt; mix them, dissolve them, and boil them; which will be done in ten or twelve Minutes.

John Nott: The Cooks and Confectioners Dictionary (1723)

— ⁓⁓⁓ —

Chocolate was traditionally made with water, both in Central America and also in Europe. In 1662 Stubbe (p. 109) attributed the making of chocolate with milk, instead of with water, to the English:

> *"Here in England we are not content with the plain Spanish way of mixing Chocolata with water: but they either use milk alone; or half milk, and half-conduit water; or else thicken the water (if they mix no water with it) with one or more eggs..."*

However, Nott's recipe, and others like it from the 18th century, show that making chocolate with water (or the knowledge of it) persisted into the 1700s.

The recipe below is based on the same proportions as Nott suggests. It makes a nice, but very different type of hot chocolate. The flavour does not linger in the mouth as long as a milk hot chocolate and it is inevitably thinner than modern versions.

— ⁓⁓⁓ —

Ingredients (makes 2)
280ml water
40g dark chocolate
25g sugar

30ml brandy
A pinch of corn flour
A pinch of salt.

Method
Put all the ingredients into a saucepan and whisk gently over a low heat until the chocolate has melted and the ingredients are combined. Bring to a gentle simmer for 2 mins, stirring constantly. Serve into warmed teacups.

To Make Wine Chocolate

TAKE a Pint of Sherry, or a Pint and half of red Port, four Ounces and a half of Chocolate, six Ounces of fine Sugar, and half an Ounce of white Starch, or fine Flour; mix, dissolve, and boil all these as before. But if your Chocolate be with Sugar, take double the Quantity of Chocolate, and half the Quantity of Sugar; and so in all.

John Nott: The Cooks and Confectioners Dictionary (1723)

— ∿∿∿∿∿ —

It was logistically difficult to obtain French wines in England during the 18th century, due to the almost constant state of war that raged between the two countries. It is less usual in England to come across references to French wine, but extremely common to see references to the Iberian fortified wines, such as Madeira, port, sherry, or sack (a type of sherry). This recipe for wine chocolate is one such recipe, however, the sweetness of these fortified wines goes extremely well with chocolate.

For the modern recipe below we have used port, but this can always be substituted for another fortified wine or a red dessert wine.

By the time the recipe quantities have been reduced to make enough for two (rather than about 20), the amount of flour that needs to be added becomes negligible. Also, the chocolate itself acts as a thickening agent and so it is not really necessary to add the flour at all.

— ∿∿∿∿∿ —

Ingredients (serves 2 in shot glasses)
100ml port   10g sugar
30g chocolate

Method
Put all the ingredients in a small saucepan and gradually bring to a gentle simmer, whisking continuously. Pour into warmed shot glasses and serve immediately.

How to Make Chocolate

TAKE six pounds of cocoa-nuts, one pound of aniseeds, four ounces of long-pepper, one of cinnamon, a quarter of a pound of almonds, one pound of pistachios, as much achiote as will make it the colour of brick, three grains of musk, and as much ambergrease, six pounds of loaf-sugar, one ounce of nutmegs, dry and beat them, and searce them through a fine sieve; your almonds must be beat to a paste, and mixed with the other ingredients; then dip your sugar in orange-flower or rose-water, and put it in a skillet, on a very gentle charcoal fire; then put it in the spice, and stew it well together, then the musk and ambergrease, then put in the cocoa-nuts last of all then achoite, wetting it with the water the sugar was dipt in; stew all these very well together over a hotter fire than before; then take it up, and put it into boxes, or what form you like and set it to dry in a warm place. The pistachios and almonds must be a little beat in a mortar, then ground upon a stone.

Hannah Glasse: The Art of Cookery Made Plain and Easy (1774)

In the 18th century chocolate bars (for making hot chocolate) were both made in the home and also bought. The recipe above is for making your own chocolate bar, however, some of the ingredients are not commonly available today, i.e. ambergrease, musk and achiote. The recipe below takes out the need for making a bar of chocolate and is for making a hot chocolate using as many of the flavours as possible that are still available today. We have not included pistachios, but you can always make a pistachio paste (the same way as the almond paste) and include that too.

Ingredients (makes 2 mugs or 4 small cups)

560ml milk
200g dark chocolate
30g almond paste/ground almonds
7g nutmeg

7g cinnamon
Pinch of ground anise seed
Pinch of long pepper
1/2tsp rose water

Method

Make your almond paste by putting ground almonds into a spice mixer or pestle and mortar and processing until paste-like. Put the paste in a saucepan over a low heat with a tablespoon of the milk and stir; adding gradually more milk until the paste is dissolved. Add the rest of the ingredients and continue whisking until all the chocolate comes to a simmer. Serve.

8

Sham Chocolate

TAKE a pint of milk, boil it over a slow fire, with some whole cinnamon, and sweeten it with Lisbon sugar; beat up the yolks of three eggs, throw all together into a chocolate pot, and mill it one way, or it will turn. Serve it up in chocolate cups.

Hannah Glasse: The Art of Cookery Made Plain and Easy (1774)

— 〰〰〰 —

This is a really interesting recipe for many reasons, it is also delicious, but do not expect it to taste of chocolate!

The idea of 'sham' foods in Georgian times, was to make food either look or taste like the real thing, whilst being made from something else. In this instance, they are going for the look of chocolate, not in colour, but in the frothy texture. It is likely that the drink was a poorer version of chocolate as not only are they making it without chocolate, but they are using a Lisbon sugar. Lisbon sugar was considered to be a poor relation to the sugar that was being imported from Jamaica and Barbados in the 18th century. It was slightly softer and not so white.

This drink is a wonderful bedtime drink that is sweet and creamy. We have slightly reduced the amount of egg, because the main breeds of hens in the 18th century laid slightly smaller eggs than our modern breeds.

— 〰〰〰 —

Ingredients (makes 1 large mug or 2 tea cups)
280ml milk
1 cinnamon stick

20g light brown sugar
1 egg yolk

Method
Put the milk, cinnamon and sugar into a saucepan and heat over a low heat until the liquid starts to simmer, whisking constantly. Remove the cinnamon stick and beat in the egg. Pour into warmed cups.

Chocolate - Food

Prior to the mid-1800s chocolate was primarily consumed as a drink. This was because the processing technology had not advanced enough to make the smooth chocolate bars that we associate with chocolate today. Bars did exist, but they were harder and grainier. The purpose of these bars was to be grated and melted, mainly to make a drink. However, the chocolate bars were also grated and melted into foods.

In Britain, by the 1700s, sweet chocolate dishes were appearing on the table. The dishes varied, but were generally consistent with other food stuffs appearing at that time. In middle to upper class households sugar and cream featured high on the list of ingredients used, both of which take on flavour, making dishes very tasty, if extremely unhealthy! Chocolate was not an exception and chocolate recipes exist for biscuits (p.13), creams (p.17), tarts (p.14 & 15) and puffs or small meringue-like delicacies (p.16).

On the continent the variety of chocolate dishes was somewhat wider, and not just restricted to sweet dishes. The French recipe for a duck stew from 1695 (p.12) uses chocolate in a way that compliments the richness of the other ingredients, making a very savoury autumnal meal. Across the Alps in northern Italy, by the 1700s chocolate was also being used in imaginative ways. The work of Don Felice Libera in the 18th century records a number of chocolate recipes, including ones for more familiar dishes like chocolate cream. He also includes some very different recipes, such as a chocolate soup served over toasted bread (p.19), which makes a lovely quick pudding. A more obscure recipe for chocolate battered omelette (p.18) is interesting and really challenges the modern boundary between sweet and savoury.

English cookery books in 18th century were becoming mass-produced and they often copied recipes verbatim from earlier editions. Chocolate recipes from hand-written recipe books do exist, for instance one for making chocolate with water in the York archives, but this is still in the same vein to other widely available books. The Don Felice Libera recipes are interesting because they are quite different, perhaps giving us a glimpse how chocolate use varied regionally.

Macreuse en ragout au Chocolat (Duck stew with chocolate)

Ayant plumé et nettoié proprement votre macreuse, vuidez-la, et la lavez, faites-la blanchir sur la braise, et ensuite empotez-la, et l'assaisonnez de sel, poivre, laurier, et un bouquet: vous ferez un peu de chocolat, que vous jetterez dedans. Preparez en meme-temps un ragout avec les foies, champignons, morilles, mousserons, truffles, un quarteron de marons; et votre Macreuse étant cuite et dressée dans son plat, versez votre ragout par-dessus et servez garni de ce que vous voudrez.

François Massialot: Le Cuisinier Royal et Bourgeois (1693)

We often think of savoury chocolate recipes as being of Central American origin, for instance the addition of chocolate into spicy meat sauce dishes, like mole. However, Massialot's early French recipe is for cooking a water fowl (we chose duck) with chocolate. It makes a lovely stew with the mushrooms, chestnuts and truffle oil giving it an autumnal earthiness.

The original recipe is not entirely clear on the cooking method. It can read that you need to roast the duck and make the rich sauce as an accompaniment, but the interpretation where all the ingredients are cooked together in a stew is certainly the most flavoursome.

Ingredients (serves 2-3)

2 duck breasts, skinned & chopped
1tbs olive oil
30g chocolate
200g chestnut mushrooms
25g porcini mushrooms
30g chestnuts, cooked and peeled

1 bay leaf
100g liver, chopped (optional)
1/2tsp of each herb: rosemary, parsley and thyme
Water.
Truffle oil (optional)

Method

Preheat the oven to 150°C. In a flameproof casserole dish, quickly fry the duck in the oil over a medium heat. Add the rest of the ingredients (except the truffle oil) and enough water to partly cover them. Bring to the boil and put in the oven to cook slowly for 2 hours. Drizzle with the truffle oil before serving.

12

Chocolate Biscuits

Take half a pound of almonds, pour boiling water over them, to rub their skins off; then set them to dry in a stove; when you take them out of the stove, and they are quite dry, pound them in a mortar with half the white of an egg; when they are well pounded put them on a plate, and take two ounces of chocolate, which you melt in a small pan over a gentle fire; when it is melted, put in your paste of almonds, mixing the whole well with a spoon; when all is well mixed, add the white of an egg and sugar, till you see your paste a little thick, and that it does not stick to your fingers...then take a rolling pin, and spread your paste on the tin plate, till you bring it to half a finger thickness. Have tin moulds of all sorts; cut your paste, and put it upon paper which lies on a sheet of tin, and place them in an oven, which should not be too hot. The smaller your tin moulds, the prettier your biscuits will look.

John Perkins: Every Woman Her Own House-Keeper (1746)

These biscuits resemble a dense, chocolatey macaroon. Recipes exist for biscuits made in a similar manner, but with different flavourings, such as lemon, almond and chocolate. In this respect, the biscuits were similar to 'puffs' and 'creams' where chocolate was just one possible variation.

We prefer to make them small, about a teaspoonful of mixture at a time, and serve them on the side with coffee.

Ingredients (makes 8-10 using a 4cm round cutter or about 20 smaller biscuits)

120g ground almonds
30g dark chocolate, broken into pieces

1 egg white
90g sugar

Method

Preheat the oven to 150°C. Line a baking sheet with grease proof paper. Melt the chocolate in a pan over a very low heat, stirring constantly. When it is melted, add the other ingredients and mix together. Roll out the mixture to 5mm thick. Use a 4cm pastry cutter to cut out your biscuits. Place them on the tray and bake for 20 mins. Transfer to a cooling rack and allow to cool completely before storing in an airtight container.

A Chocolate Tart

TAKE a quarter of a pound of rasped chocolate, a stick of cinnamon, some fresh lemon-peel grated, a little salt and some sugar; take two spoonfuls of fine flour, the yolks of six eggs well beat and mixed with some milk; put all these into a stew-pan, and let them be a little while over the fire; then put in a little preserved lemon-peel cut small, and let it stand to be cold; beat up the whites of eggs, enough to cover it, put it in puff-paste: when it is baked, sift some sugar over and glaze it with a salamander.

J. Walter: The Lady's Assistant for Regulating and Supplying the Table (1787)

—◦◦◦◦◦—

This chocolate tart shares many similarities with the Tourte de Chocolate (p.15), however, it does vary in two ways. The first is that it uses milk rather than cream, which gives it a rich, but a slightly lighter texture. Secondly, the richness of this dish is balanced very nicely with the acidity of the fresh lemon peel and the preserved, or candied, lemon peel.

This really is a dish that would be perfectly at home at any modern dinner party.

—◦◦◦◦◦—

Ingredients (serves 6-8)

120g dark chocolate, in small pieces
1 cinnamon stick
Grated peel of 1 lemon
A pinch of salt
30g sugar, and extra for glazing
1tbs corn flour

3 egg yolks, beaten and whites, reserved
230ml whole milk
15g candied lemon peel
320g Ready-rolled puff pastry

Method

Preheat the oven to 180°C. Blind bake the pastry in a 22cm flan tin with a removable base for 25 mins. Meanwhile, make the filling for the tart by putting the chocolate, cinnamon, grated lemon peel, salt, sugar, flour, eggs and milk in a pan and heating gradually over a low heat, whisking frequently. When combined and starting to thicken, remove from the heat, add the candied lemon peel and allow to cool. Then, whisk the egg whites to stiff peaks. Fill the pastry case with the chocolate mixture and top with egg white, sprinkle sugar over the top. Turn the oven down to 150°C and bake for 45 mins. Allow to cool completely, before serving.

To Make a Tourte de Chocolate

MIX a little flour with a pint of cream, and chocolate in proportion, a little sugar, and four eggs; boil it about a quarter of an hour, stirring it continually for fear it should catch at bottom; then put it in the paste, and the whites of four eggs beat to a snow upon it ; glaze it with sugar, and bake it.

George Dalrymple: The Practice of Modern Cookery (1781)

—✓✓✓✓✓—

This recipe makes a beautiful chocolate tart, with a meringue-type topping. The filling is rich and not too sweet, with the texture of a ganache. The egg white topping adds a contrasting colour and texture to the dish; when it is baked it is almost chewy.

Like many historic recipes, phrases such as 'in proportion' and 'a little' are used without quantifying specific amounts or time. If you prefer a sweeter filling add more sugar to the chocolate cream before you pour it into the pastry case.

—✓✓✓✓✓—

Ingredients (serves 8)

230g short-crust pastry
1 tbs flour
570ml double cream

20g chocolate
8 eggs
60g sugar, plus extra for sprinkling

Method

Roll out the pastry to cover a 22cm tin and blind bake it at 190° C for 15 mins. Combine the chocolate, 4 eggs, sugar, flour & cream in a heavy-based pan and heat slowly, stirring often until it starts to thicken. Whisk 4 egg whites to stiff peaks. Pour the chocolate into the pastry case, top with the egg whites, sprinkle sugar over the top & bake at 150°C for 45 mins. Wait 15 mins before serving if serving hot. This dish can be served hot or cold.

To make Chocolate Puffs

BEAT and sift half a pound of double refined sugar, scrape into it one ounce of chocolate very fine, mix them together, beat the white of an egg to a very high froth, then strew in your sugar and chocolate; keep beating it till it is as stiff as paste, sugar your papers, and drop them on about the size of a sixpence, and bake them in a very slow oven.

Elizabeth Raffald: The Experienced English Housekeeper (1786)

—〰〰〰—

'Puffs' were a popular 18th century dish and recipes for different flavours occur in many of the cookery books from this period. It is common to find recipes for chocolate puffs, lemon puffs, sugar puffs and almond puffs.

Puffs are essentially small, very sweet meringues. They probably would have been served as a corner dish as part of the second course, or with the dessert course at a Georgian dining table in a middle to upper class household.

Some recipes call for grated or powdered chocolate that has been sifted. This recipe does not ask for the chocolate to be sifted and the finished effect is one of a coffee-coloured meringue with dark chocolate flecks.

—〰〰〰—

Ingredients (makes approx. 15-20 small puffs)
225g icing sugar   1 egg white
30g dark chocolate, grated

Method
Preheat the oven to 140°C. Line a baking tray with grease proof paper. Sift the icing sugar into a bowl and stir in the chocolate. In a separate bowl, whisk the egg white until it forms stiff peaks. Gradually whisk in the sugar and chocolate, until it forms a stiff paste, you might need to swap to using a wooden spoon. Put dollops of mixture, the size of a ten pence piece, onto the tray. Bake for 20-30 mins.

To make Chocolate Cream

Take a quart of cream, a pint of white wine and a little juice of lemon; sweeten it well, lay in a sprig of rosemary, grate some chocolate and mix altogether; stir it over the fire until it is thick; and pour it into your cups.

Hannah Glasse: The Complete Confectioner (1800)

— ∿∿∿ —

This recipe makes a set chocolate cream that is thick and rich, similar to the *petits pots de crème au chocolat* that you find in France today.

In a similar way to the Chocolate Tart (p. 14) this recipe has some slightly acidic flavours in it. The combination of the sweet white wine and the lemon juice adds a fruity, slightly tangy, kick to this rich dessert.

This is another recipe that would sit comfortably on the table at a modern dinner party as a dessert. In Georgian times it would have probably have been served as part of the second course along with other creams, jellies and syllabubs. Indeed, the ingredients of this dish, minus the chocolate, are very similar to a syllabub, hinting at the possible origins of this dish.

— ∿∿∿ —

Ingredients (serves 6 in small wine glasses or espresso cups)

280ml double cream
140ml sweet white wine
50g dark chocolate

50g sugar
1tsp lemon juice
A sprig of rosemary

Method

Put all the ingredients in a saucepan and heat gently, whisking constantly until all the chocolate has melted and the colour is like milk chocolate, rather than grainy. Once the chocolate has melted, let the liquid come to a gentle simmer for 1 min. Remove the rosemary, pour the chocolate between the glasses or cups, allow to cool and then chill for at least four hours or until set.

Frittura che potra servire da grasso, e da magro
(Chocolate-battered omelette)

Fate una Frittata secondo il solito, e fatela grande a misura delle persone, che dovete servire; indi versatela sopra una tavola pulita, e quando sarà fredda, tagliatela allora in fette a modo Fegato; poscia immergete queste fette ad una nella cioccolata preparata già, e fatta secondo il solito; indi involgetele nella farina di formento, e poi immergetele di nuovo nella detta cioccolata, e dopo ancora involgetele nella suddetta farina; indi fatele subito friggere nel butirro fresco ben caldo a modo di Fegato; e quando saranno colorite da tutte due le parti, allora servitele in Tavola calde.

Don Felice Libera: L'arte della Cucina, ricette di cibi e di dulci (Mid-late 18th century) in Mazzoni (ed.) 1986

—〰〰〰—

This is one of the strangest foods we have come across. The little strips of chocolate-battered omelette look like strips of beef, but have a crunchy outer layer and a soft omelette centre. It appears to be a savoury dish, with the chocolate adding to the overall richness. The recipe's context in the original book reveals little about how it was eaten. It appears in a section of fried dishes, such as: fried apple or pear, fried rice, fried veal and fried brains!

—〰〰〰—

Ingredients (serves 4)
2 eggs, whisked
A knob of butter
25g chocolate
100ml milk

10g sugar
100g flour
50g butter

Method
Heat the knob of butter in a small frying pan. Add the whisked eggs and cook as you would a normal omelette. Allow the omelette to cool and then it cut into strips between 0.5 - 1cm thick. Put the chocolate, milk and sugar in a small pan over a low heat and whisk until all the ingredients are combined. Then soak the omelette strips in the chocolate, toss them in flour, dip them in chocolate and toss them in the flour again. Heat the remaining butter in a large frying pan and fry the chocolate-covered omelette strips over a high heat until browned. Serve.

Zuppa cioccolata
(Chocolate Soup)

Ponete in una padella della farina di formento, e andatela mescolando sopra il fuoco sino, che avra preso colore di Cioccolata; poscia levatela dal fuoco, e passate questa farina per lo staccio; indi ponete in altra padella di ottone un picciolo cucchiajo della suddetta farina, un poco di canella pestata, zucchero, un pezzetto di Cioccolate, e tanto sale come se aveste a salare un uovo fresco, e sciogliete ogni cosa con un quarto di mossa di latte; poi fatela bollire per lo spazio di tre minuti, mescolandola sempre sin a tanto, che alza il bollo dopo levate dal fuoco la padella, e continuate a mescolare; e quando la mescola, colla quale mescolate, sara quasi come verniciata, allora subito versate questa composizione sopra le fette di pane abbrustolate.

Don Felice Libera: L'arte della Cucina, ricette di cibi e di dulci (Mid-late 18th century) in Mazzoni (ed.) 1986

—∿∿∿∿∿—

This Italian recipe makes a dish that resembles something between a chocolatey French toast and bread pudding. It is a very good way to soften hard or slightly stale bread, as the chocolate 'soup' soaks into the toast. It makes a quick pudding or a decadent breakfast
.

Like all of Libera's recipes, this dish does not appear in other mainstream European cookery books from the period.

—∿∿∿∿∿—

Ingredients (serves 4)
75g chocolate, broken into pieces   400ml milk
1/2tsp corn flour   1 egg yolk, beaten
1tsp cinnamon   Slices of toast to serve four.
Pinch of salt

Method
Put the chocolate, corn flour, cinnamon and salt into a saucepan and heat gently, stirring constantly over a low heat until the chocolate is melted. Gradually stir in the milk. Once the milk and chocolate are combined, turn up the heat and bring to a simmer, stirring frequently. Simmer for 3 mins, remove from the heat. Stir in the egg yolk and continue to cook, while stirring, until the consistency is like paint. Pour over slices of toast and serve immediately.

Notes

Chocolate
We have used a good quality dark chocolate for creating all the recipes in this book. We would recommend using a chocolate with at least 70% cocoa solids, as not only is this more authentic, but the addition of milk or cream in a lot of the recipes would water down a milk chocolate too much.

Conversions
All conversions into metric are approximate. The recipes were originally written in 'pounds and ounces'.

Authors' Information

Suzi Richer has a PhD in Environmental Archaeology and is particularly interested in how people produced food in the past. She has worked for the National Trust and has published articles in both popular and academic publications. She enjoys experimenting with historic recipes and recreating flavours from the past.

Nick Trustram Eve is an historic interpreter specialising in bringing the past to life through the senses, particularly in relation to food. He is specifically interested in the Tudor and Georgian periods and gives talks and demonstrations on period foods and dining. Nick has worked for the National Trust and with other heritage organisations providing interpretation. He also produces a range of historic foods for modern consumption for his historic food business, The Copper Pot.

The Copper Pot
A selection of products produced by The Copper Pot are available to purchase at: **www.thecopperpot.co.uk**, including a range of historic hot chocolate mixes.

Acknowledgements

Many thanks to Giovanna Bellandi for her help with the Italian translations and to Lyn Richer for proof reading.

Bibliography

Dalrymple, G (1781) *The Practice of Modern Cookery.*

Glasse, H (1774) *The Art of cookery Made Plain and Easy.*

Glasse, H (1800) *The Complete Confectioner.*

Massialot, F (1693) *Le Cuisinier Royal et Bourgeois.*

Mazzoni, A (ed) (1986) *L'Arte della Cucina: ricette di cibi e di dolci di Don Felice Libera.* Testi Antichi di Gastronomia No. 19. Sala Bolognese: Arnaldo Forni.

Nott, J (1723) *The Cook's and Confectioner's Dictionary: or the Accomplish'd Housewife's Companion.*

Perkins, J (1746) *Every Woman Her Own House-Keeper.*

Raffald, E (1786) *The Experienced English Housekeeper.* London: Baldwin.

Sheridan, T (1789) A Complete Dictionary of the English Language, Both with Regard to Sound and Meaning: Vol 1. 2nd edn.

Stubbe, H (1662) *The Indian Nectar, or A Discourse concerning Chocolata.* London: Andrew Crook at the sign of the Green Dragon).

Walter, J (1787) *The Lady's Assistant for Regulating and Supplying the Table.*